HE LOVES ME!

HE LOVES ME NOT!

Confessions of A Cheater

CONFESSIONS

OF A

CHEATER

Ten Ways To Make Your Man Love You

By: VINCENT A. WILLIAMS

Confessions of A Cheater

CONFESSIONS OF A CHEATER...... (Ten Ways 2 Make Your Man Love U)

Copyright © 2011 by Vincent Williams

Pieces of Me Publishing © 2011
Piecesofme33@yahoo.com

Contact information:

vincentwilliams2@student.owens.edu

419-701-8242

DEDICATION

This book is dedicated to all the women I hurt in my life. Yes, even you. In this book I will explain all the mistakes you made while we were together. I will also explain why I did the things I did. How many men do you know will admit this? As you continue to read you will understand why I had to write this book. I can't justify the things I've done and won't dare try to.

I also want to dedicate this book to my sisters, cousins, aunties, friends and all the women in this world who have been hurt by men. Hopefully you will become more aware of why men do what they do.

I know a lot of men will be mad at me. Hell, I may even lose the respect of some friends. In the long run this book may help save some men too. See, if a man has a good, strong woman at home who knows her worth; that may limit him from making some bad decisions. Men, you don't want to lose a great woman. Maybe instead of making a bunch of foolish choices, like robbing, cheating, or even killing, you will think about the value of that woman that's not worth losing. Women, you have way more power than you know.

The main and most important reason I wrote this book is for my heart, my daughter, Deija Jynell Lee Williams. She is twelve years old and I don't want her making the same mistakes I see women making every day. A couple of my ex. girlfriends have said that Deija is going to end up with a man just like me. Deija has seen some of my struggles with women and I've told her not to ever let a man mistreat her. She says she never will. Hopefully through this book, God will spare my daughter from having her heart broken by men, despite all the hearts that I've broken.

Last but not least I want to dedicate this book to my sons; Vincent Jr., Michauen and Stylez. I want them to know how to treat the woman in their lives. Don't do what your dad did.

Confessions of A Cheater

TABLE OF CONTENTS

PREFACE

One day my brother came over my house, and said "bro let's make a face book page!" My response was, No! I am not getting caught up in that internet world. My brother convinced me that it was all for fun. Of course my girl had something to say about it; but I said "let's do it!" When I got on face book I realized I had a lot of family & friends that I haven't spoken too in awhile. Before I knew it I had over 200 friends in the first 4 days.

I have a big family, and mostly girls, and every day they ask me questions about relationships. So, I decided to post a comment every week to help people. I called it **"Thought of the Week"**. People would tell me *"Thanks for that thought of the week, it was inspirational and please keep those thoughts coming."* My sister called me and said, she was having a hard time with her man problems. Soon after her my cousins began calling. Then one day an old friend called me with her man problems. After giving her advice she said these words to me that sort of struck something within, she said: "Vince you should write a book because you always helping people with their problems." After hearing that comment it hit me and I thought hmm, I should write a short book. As a matter of fact, I will write a book, a book on how to make your man love you.

At first it was just for my sister's and friends and now it expanded to all women. I'm pretty sure the men will have something to say because of the unwritten men law that all men just automatically know. Basically don't give the women the game let them be blind to our secrets, but after seeing my sister get hurt by her husband, I said, THAT'S IT! Not another one of my female relatives should be hurt by another man.

I asked my sister what she considers an expert. She said; I don't know! My definition of an expert is a person with a lot of experience in one typical field. So let's see I've been playing poker for 6 years, and I've been studying criminal justice for 2 years, also study business for a year. I've been a grown man for 13 years and learning to become a man for 30 years therefore, I would consider myself an expert at understanding and knowing a man. So, I told my sister's this **"never let a man run game on you when you know that you have a brother who can direct you step by step."**

ACKNOWLEDGEMENTS

First of all I would like to thank God because none of this would be possible without him. "Thank you God, I love you!"

A special thanks to my mom, Ruby Quinceanna Williams. I wouldn't be here without you. I love you to death. I promised you a while ago that I was going to buy you a house. That promise will not be broken.

Thank you so much to my editor, LaToya Williams (CEO of "Pieces of Me" Publishing House). You really put in some work helping me get this project off the ground. I love you cousin.

Thanks to my models, Christina Moorer (my sister), Sandy Singkham (my son mother), Marabeth Guillen (friend), and Antonia (Lady) Williams (my cousin)

Thanks to my photographer (Doitwithlove photography)

ADVISORY:

Some of the words and contents in this book may not be suitable for children.

INTRODUCTION

Do you ever wonder why men are so good in the beginning?

Let me tell you why. If they show you who they really are, they know you won't waste your time.

My parable is this; both a man and a woman are like an orange. See, a man is an orange with the skin still on it; you know you got to peel the orange before you get to the actual fruit.

Now,   once you peel it, you taste the sweet and softness of an orange. That's exactly how a man is; you must peel the skin off before you actually get to the person. A man may act hard and careless, but in reality once you get pass the peel, you find out how soft and sensitive a man really is. Once he falls in love with you, he doesn't want to show you all his real feelings, because you may not know, but he knows that you are the strength to the relationship and he really can't do it without you.

A woman is also like an orange but one that has already been peeled; she's not as likely to hide her feelings. She automatically shows the man how she feels for him. A woman shows her soft and sensitive side in the beginning and that's when a man takes advantage. If you women would just learn how to hold back just a little and cover up your feelings with the orange peelings. Take your time before you show a man how you really feel and there will be more women getting married and less women that are staying with men who are beneath their level.

Have you ever seen a woman with a man, and you say; "what is she doing with him?" Well that man covered up his real self with his orange peels and showed the woman his macho and how hard he is. In contrast, that woman gave that man her natural self way too early. A man knows once he gets to that heart he can reveal himself because now she's not going anywhere. Men have been doing this for years. That's why it's important that women take their time and learn who their man really is before they give in.

Don't wait until after two or three kids are involved to find out he isn't about nothing. **LEARN HIM BEFORE YOU GIVE IN!** So men strap on your seatbelts and women enjoy the ride. This is; "Confessions of a Cheater (Ten ways 2 make your man love you)

WARNING:

ENTER AT YOUR OWN RISK (YOU WILL COME OUT WITH A DIFFERENT MIND SET)

CHAPTER

1

HOW

DO

I KNOW

IF MY MAN

IS

CHEATING

In this chapter, I want you to recognize the signs of your man cheating. Also the steps that your man takes to break you down that will eventually result in you accepting his immature ways.

HE LOVES ME

Women, it's real simple to find out if your man is cheating. See, I'm just like you, the average guy next door, so you won't see any real big words that you can't understand. I will be very **bold** and make it very easy to understand how to make your man love you.

There is one device that has all the answers to your questions; **CELL PHONE.** If you are allowed to answer your man cell phone, that is a great sign that your man is not cheating. Don't get me wrong, these days men have gotten a lot smarter. Some men will have another line hidden, so don't put them in the clear just yet.

For example: IF your man sleeps with his phone under his pillow, then **he has something to hide**. Now, if and when you are with your man and his phone stays glued to his hip, or when he's away from you, he hesitates to answer it, **that should be a red flag to you immediately.**

See the problem is most women know their man is cheating but they put up with him for various reasons. I'll explain those later on in the chapters. Growing up I was told that women were the best investigators, so use your GOD-given ability. Look for signs when your man comes around. A very normal thing that men do is, reward you with gifts like roses, and cards, or massages, some even cook dinner. These can be signs of your man cheating. Don't get me wrong there are men who are just nice, sweet, and sensitive. Who just like to spoil their woman but you need to recognize that in the beginning. A man may have just left from seeing his other lady and you may already be suspicious. Suddenly he walks in with roses; it automatically makes you forget that **he didn't answer your calls earlier.**

Another sign to recognize is this; **does your man take you out in public a lot?** The majority of cheaters do not go out in public with their girl a lot because it limits them to women, **although there are women who thrive on sleeping with married men and men who are in a relationship.** Yet, a cheater doesn't want to limit his choices, besides he might run into the one that can **replace you** if you don't complete him.

HERE IS THE REMEDY TO CHANGING A CHEATER

Set your demands early in a relationship! What I mean is this; in the beginning of a relationship man put women through numerous of test to see what she will allow him to get away with.

Example, A man might say "baby let's have a threesome" just to get a reaction out of you. If this is your response, **"Baby quit playing, you so silly, with who? You know I don't get down like that no boo strictly dick."** The next time he may start asking you questions like; Babe so you think she's pretty? He may also say, would you go down on a pretty female or would you let her go down on you? The questions will keep coming until he breaks you down. Before you know it, you have slept with a woman; something you never thought you would do.

Your response should have been a lot different, something like this; **"I don't know who the hell you thought I was, don't you ever disrespect me like that again, Bye go find you a whore because whore is not in my resume."** Or even immediately end the relationship to show him you mean business and there are no games when it comes to your heart.

That's what I mean by setting your demands early. You have to **check your man immediately** and that's how you gain your respect in your relationship. See, when you respond that way your man has to respect you. He won't try to get away with disrespectful gestures like this one word that some men love to call their woman: **Bitch!**

Never let your man call you a bitch! Men are very slick with throwing that word in. A male's **ego** is so huge, and he definitely wants to show his friends that he has his woman in check. It makes him feel powerful and like he's somebody. The first time he calls you a bitch you **check him like this; "who the HELL you talking to like that, don't you ever call me that again."** Some women even resort to a violent attack. Now I don't recommend for any woman to be assaulting a man. Let's not forget that he's a man, but that was a good response; because you checked him instantly. Now, if he calls you a **bitch** while you guys are playing and you laugh at it; **BIG MISTAKE!**

Do you see the process? He is slowly breaking you down. Before you know it every little comment will end with the word bitch, followed by a little giggle behind it. Next thing you know, **your name is bitch,** now everywhere you go he's calling you a bitch. Your response should have been "listen baby I don't care what's going on, serious or playing, don't ever call me a bitch again, okay. I am telling you nicely now because I have way too much respect for myself to allow anyone to call me anything other than my name." His response will be "**my bad baby I apologize** to you and it will never happen again."

Now let's get back to the main subject in this chapter; **cheating**. Men use a lot of different tactics to get out of a conversation when it comes to cheating. Here's a couple that you may have heard before. **"What; you don't trust me, or the all famous, you so insecure."**

For some reason women let those words make them feel guilty. No! Your response should be, **"If I'm insecure it's because you made me this way."** What if it's a brand new relationship and he says you're too insecure? Your response should be this; "baby when it comes to my heart I am very protective and if you want to win my heart these are the necessary steps you have to take to get there. If it's too much for you then maybe I'm not the one for you." When you respond that way you're telling him you are a real woman and you know your worth. If he's going to be with you; he has to come **CORRECT!**

Here is one of my favorite quotes that I like to use; **"You have two ears and one mouth. Listen twice as much as you speak."** The point I'm trying to make is; just listen to people who have more experience with relationships, so you won't have to experience it by yourself. Some people are not strong enough to deal with heartbreak. How many suicides have you heard of from a broken heart? If you listen twice as much as you speak you will more than likely learn from listening. This will lessen your chance physically experiencing a broken heart.

DON'T GIVE UP THE GOODS UNTIL HE IS EXCLUSIVELY YOUR MAN!

As I come to a close of this chapter I'm going to let you know about a major mistake that women seem to always do when they are with a man. NEVER AND I MEAN NEVER (like Smokey says in the movie "Friday") "NEVER EVER, EVER, EVER" SLEEP WITH A MAN THAT YOU **"REALLY LIKE"** BEFORE BECOMING HIS WOMAN. Some like to call it friends with benefits, but trust me if you ever want him to become your man, it will never happen. You ever heard the saying; **"why buy the cow when you can get the milk for free?"** Well that's exactly what I am saying.

If he is sleeping with you and doing all the things that you would do in a real relationship then **you are wasting your time if you ever think he will be your man.** You are just a **side chick** and will remain a side chick, unless you **change things yourself**. The remedy to going from a side chick to a main chick is to **CUT HIM OFF**! What I mean by cutting him off is to stop doing all the womanly duties. Cooking, massages, errands, etc. all the things you do for him, **STOP**! That's the only way he will even recognize how important you are. He **won't** change until you do that.

See when a woman does all the things for a man who is not hers he becomes very spoiled and use to it. To the point where he will make you feel obligated to do what he says. So if you want things to be different those things you use to do for him; you have to make him do them himself. This way he will start missing you and he will definitely start comparing you to his main chick. Basically, completely cut him off until he starts **begging** (and trust me, he will start begging) you to come around then you're breaking him down. See, a man really loves a woman but the majority of men won't let the woman know how he really feels. He hides his emotions from you with aggression, lies, cuss words, abusive words, and sometimes physical abuse.

He only does this because he knows that **if you (the woman) ever realize how much power you really have in the relationship you will have complete control over everything he does.** Now don't get me wrong I am not trying to break up happy homes but if this is your situation and your man has a chick on the side then your house is not a happy home after all. For the main chick if you want to keep your man from even having **"side chicks"** don't be scared to get a little creative with your relationship. **Cheat "on" your man "with" your man.** Sometimes be your own alter ego, (Police Woman, Naughty Teacher, Innocent School Girl, Naughty Nurse and whoever else you want) keep the spice in the relationship. Therefore, he has no reason to go out and cheat because you're doing everything yourself.

Also, with you keeping the relationship fresh and brand new, he doesn't know who he's coming home to. But I tell you this; he **WILL** be home every night waiting to see who you're going to be portraying next.

Have you ever watched any of the movies with Madea in them where Madea is actually played by a man name Tyler Perry? Well, Tyler Perry is killing two birds with one stone; everyone knows Tyler Perry is a Christian and a strong believer of God. So, he dresses like a crazy ass old lady. He says and does all the crazy things he wants to do as "Madea" but when he's Tyler he does the complete opposite. He knows that a crazy old woman will be hilarious and will sell more tickets than if he's just being himself. All the while, deep down inside, you and I both know that he wants to say and do some of those things as Tyler Perry. Instead, he uses his alter ego (Madea) and keeps Tyler Perry out of the hot seat and in the bank. This not anything bad against Tyler Perry (at all). My point is this; in your relationship be your own alter ego. Do everything you really want to do as yourself but may be too afraid to do it because of fear of your lover not liking or accepting it. **LET YOUR "ALTER EGO" be the tool you use to BE FREE!**

REMEMBER:

If he is sleeping with you and doing all the things that you would do in a real relationship then you are wasting your time if you think he will ever be your man.

HE LOVES ME NOT

CHAPTER

2

HOW

DO I GET

MORE

CONTROL

OVER MY

RELATIONSHIP

In this chapter, I want you to recognize that you can have control in your relationship and that is totally up to you. It's all about knowing who you are and making sure that he understands that you know who you are.

Well, the way of having control in your relationship is to never give it up. You have control in the beginning for the simple fact that the **majority of men approach the woman.** Now, that man doesn't know if you're feeling him or not. Maybe a couple insecure women blew his head up or what we like to say; "gassed his head up" so now he's feeling confident enough to approach you.

At this time, your conversation is important. There is nothing wrong with a hood chick but your vocabulary lets a man know how to approach you. If he approaches with one of these lines "What's good baby, Hey sexy, Dam mama you cold as hell, or the famous, where your man at?" In return, you respond like this; "What's up daddy, or hey Sexy, I don't have a man," then instantly he's going to think that you're not going to be a hard task. Your response should be; "Dam, that's how you were taught to approach a lady? Thank you!" and keep going. "My man is at home getting my dinner ready." That response automatically let's him know that he's dealing with a **confident and mature woman**. You've expressed that you have received a compliment before. If he's fine or your type, that alone will make him try harder.

See men have different levels of game they like to use. It's a C game, B game and then you have the A game. Now it's sad to say but your appearance lets him know which game to use when he approaches you. Next is your conversation, so how you respond will determine which level of game he will need to use. Now **A-game** is him being honest and I mean completely honest. He will tell you if he's married, got a girlfriend or whatever. He may even say "I'm seeing someone, but it's complicated." If you're still interested, then he knows he got you where he wants you. That alone should've made you walk away. Once you walk away he puts you in the **"wifey material"** category. Most women would have stayed, especially if he is "swagged" up. Now he is comparing you with his main girl at home. Thus, from this point on you have control over this whole situation. What happens next is up to you. **C-game** is when he sees that you are so into him that he doesn't have to say much. In this case, your **body language** is letting him know that he won't have to work very hard to get you. The **B-game** is basically him counter acting off of you. Whatever you say; he agrees with. If you just want to exchange numbers, he's going to act like that's all he wants to do. If you want to leave together the same night you met, he's going to be willing to do that too. He will respond **"yes"** to whatever it is that you want to do. This is the scheme of him telling you exactly what you want to hear.

Now that we got that out of the way, let's focus more on being in a relationship and keeping the control. In all reality no woman wants a man she can just control; where's the fun in that? So, you want balance but never give him the upper hand. **Again you keep balance and control over your relationship by setting your demands early in the relationship.**

You have to check your man every time he gets out of line. Remember men run women through a lot of tests but it's up to you to recognize the test and ace them with flying colors. For instance when you check your man about the little things he won't even try the big things. **Also, remember checking your man doesn't necessarily have to be a bad or mean thing.** You can check your man in a very nice and respectful way. In fact, that will be the best way; you don't ever want him to feel like he's not a man.

For example, if he says "Baby I'll be

in late tonight. **Right there!** You need to ask him around what time. Not that he's going to give you an exact time but at least you have some idea around what time he'll be home. On the other hand, your response probably shouldn't be; "okay, be safe, or love you babe." I'm not saying that's a bad response but that gives him lee-way to stay out as late as he wants. What your response should have been was; "What time do you think you'll be back? **I'LL WAIT UP FOR YOU!**" That right there will take away any chance of him coming in too late and having some lame excuse of why he did.

Another very important lesson in a relationship is being complete within your own self. What I mean by that and you see it more these days than ever, is; to be an **independent woman**. Have your own car, house, money, friends, etc… This way your whole life is not revolving around him. You ever been in a relationship and then when it was over you felt lost like you had no friends or nothing. That's because you dedicated your whole life to this man and forgot that **you should have a life as well**.

When you have your own, you make better decisions? Like; if your man isn't acting right you won't need to stay with him for monetary security. How many women stay with their man because he provides transportation, shelter, money etc? **When you don't have your own it gives him all the control of the relationship.**

So, basically the way to having more control of your relationship or to just be equal is to be WHOLE. Did you ever watch the show *"What Chilli Wants?"* Well, she gets a lot of backlash because she has a checklist but in reality that's exactly how aggressive you have to be with protecting your heart. A man knows exactly what type of woman he has if he grabs a hold to a woman like Chilli. She set her standards high and make her demands very clear early in the relationship. That's how important her heart is to her. If you take a close look at Chilli; she is a successful musical artist. So with that being said, she's in a position to **make better decisions** without needing the security of a man.

I know a lot of people may disagree with her checklist but if you were complete (as far as security goes) in all areas. As a woman you could take your time and pick and choose the man you want. So in this chapter we're learning to set your demands early, and most definitely be complete as a woman. You do this and you will not only have balance in your relationship but you will have a name/title in your relationship and not just "John's Girl."

Has that ever happened to you?

Someone approaches you not by your name but by "John's Girl." Well that's the result when your whole life is dedicated to your man. As for Chilli you hang in there and you will be married soon. The right man is out there for you. I pray that you don't ever give in or settle. Keep your checklist because if you settle women all over the world will believe a checklist is just too much. See when Chilli does find true love she will prove to all women that you don't ever have to settle and you can be patient.

PATIENCE IS A VIRTUE!

I am very picky too when it comes to being in a relationship. I think we all have a checklist mine is; no smoking, no kids, good reputation, exclusive, thick but not too thick. Anywhere from 150 to 175 pounds, it depends on height. I also prefer either black or exotic looking women. Now, I do usually stay with my own race but I'm not a racist, I have dated plenty of other races, although I was never really 100% serious with the other races. **Why?** I just really didn't have a lot in common with them.

I have dated Asian, White, Latina, and a lot of bi-racial and black women. I learned something different from every one of them. These statements may not apply to "ALL" women, but they definitely describe the ones that I've dated. This is strictly based off my own experience.

Asian women are very loyal to their man. It may be a cultural thing, I'm not sure but I was with her for 7 years. They're very committed to their family and relationship. They are also great lovers and have orgasms like none other.

White women goal is to please their man. Some white women love black men. The rumor is because black men are usually packing (if you know what I mean). These particular white women will do anything for their men. I mean anything and they tend to be very naïve. What seems to attract black men to white women is the fact that they are so giving and they love to give their man oral sex. Probably more than any other race and not only do they like to do it, but they appear to be very well trained at it (no lie).

So if you ever wonder why that black men is with her and not you, then ask yourself; **are you willing to do some of the things that the white girl is doing?**

Latina women, more often than not are great cooks and excellent lovers. They also may love to drink and party.

Bi-racial women tend to be more like the race that they're most accustomed to.

So, I prefer **black women** because we tend to have more in common. My point I am trying to make is this; it's my checklist and my life. What's wrong with me having a preference on what type of woman I want for myself? **NOTHING!** The same goes for you, **don't settle**! If you want a millionaire with no kids who's Asian with a gigantic penis, **go for it!** You might be waiting a while to find him but it's your life and I recommend that you don't settle.

Now I don't mean to offend any women of any race and don't think my book won't help you because I prefer black women. I'm just trying to show you that you need to have a checklist too. I think by dating all these different races help me to write this book. Each of these women taught me something. Those experiences helped me make a decision that when I do decide to get married it will probably be with a black woman. However you know the saying **"the heart wants what the heart wants."** Mind you, even though I prefer to be with a black woman, some of my best friends are white women. Some I've been friends with for 5 years some even 15 years and would help them if they ever needed me.

Enough about me and my checklist let's get back to yours. When it comes to looking for a man, and I'm talking about the man that you want to spend the rest of your life with; you need a checklist. Now if you just want to have fun then this book is not for you. But if you want your man to love you then continue to read.

REMEMBER:

When you don't have your own it gives him all the control of the relationship.

In the last two chapters you learned to set your demands early, be a complete woman, have a checklist, and never-ever sleep with a man that you really like before becoming his woman.

HE LOVES ME

CHAPTER

3

WHY DOES

MY MAN

TREAT ME

SO BAD

In this chapter I want you to recognize that all men are sweet in the beginning. Whatever he is will soon be revealed through his actions. There is ALWAYS a way out of an abusive relationship.

UNFORTUNATELY, THE REAL REASON YOUR MAN TREATS YOU SO BAD IS BECAUSE YOU LET HIM

A man can only do what you allowed him to do. See, a man will be the sweetest man in the beginning, even a man who beat his woman, or one who's a straight DOG. He has to give you the most appealing bait. Once he gets your attention he'll just start winding you in like a fish. It's sad to say that some men who don't even beat their women or treat them bad, begin to just because of what the woman put up with. Like I said in an earlier chapter; men put women threw a lot of tests in the beginning of the relationship. He can even be a good man, but when he says shut up bitch, or slaps you, even just playing around, your reaction to that, will determine what he will do next.

In addition, with that been said women who are being treated so bad in their relationship didn't respond the correct way in the beginning. That's why it's so important to recognize all the tests men put you through and how to respond to it. Plenty of women fight and pray for a relationship to work that GOD is trying to get rid of. **Do**

you believe every man is a blessing from GOD? Well I hope not because just like GOD can bless you the enemy is working to.

Have you ever heard about a woman meeting a very wealthy man, who is very handsome and just does all the right things? Then after awhile you hear how that woman was beaten or sometimes even murdered. Do you think GOD will bless you with a man who will beat or kill you? No way! If GOD blesses you with someone you will be truly happy and they will lead you to a closer relationship with GOD, not away from GOD. My point here is sometimes you have to just **let it go**. GOD may have something better waiting on you and he can't even bless you with him because you keep holding on to the enemy's counterfeit blessing. Not to get all religious on you but I am a firm believer of GOD.

Women tend to stay in abusive relationships for numerous of reasons. Some feel no one else will love them, or they can't make it on their own. I probably can name 20 other reasons why women stay in abusive relationships but I'll just get to my point. An abusive mans' main job is not to abuse you physically. His main job is to abuse you mentally. **He wants to brainwash you from**

your values, and replace your thoughts with his thoughts. This is why it's so important to be whole as a woman. That man will continue to call you things like; ugly, fat, insecure, bitch, slut, whore, and anything else to break you down. If he can, he'll break you to the point that you'll start thinking you deserve to be treated so badly.

How do I get out of this relationship?

You have to **find yourself** and remember who you are, therefore understanding your worth. Eject the CD that your abusive man has placed in your head and put a new one in. Get out and find you a job, go stay with family, go back to school, call the police and file charges whatever it takes. **Stand up for yourself.**

What if I have kids with this man?

Then you really want to get away because you don't want your kids to grow up and think this is the way they're suppose to be treated. You've got to change the trend. Tina Turner had to stand up to Ike. I know we all heard that story. **A man who beats a woman is very weak minded.** It could have been something he seen as a kid. So you (Woman) have to break the cycle before your kids experience the same thing.

Sometimes women are comfortable so they stick around. What I mean is, they love their home that the abusive man has provided or the name brand clothes, fancy cars, so they think the abuse comes with the territory. **Ladies, no man should ever beat you and you accept it.** That's why you make sure to take your time with any man you get with. Pay close attention to the signs he gives you in the beginning when you first meet him. **Be complete within yourself so if you ever run across an abusive man you can leave with no problem.**

You ever hear the saying don't leave a 80% good man for that other 20%. Well I agree with that some of the time, but if in that 80%, abuse is involved leave immediately. The first time your man slap you, kids or no kids, you **LEAVE.** If you feel uncomfortable with your man, **LEAVE.** If he screams at you with a rage you've never seen before, **LEAVE**. The reason you leave is because once he hits you the first time he will continue to hit you for the rest of your relationship until either one of you is dead.

What if I'm so in love with him that I can't leave?

If that is the case, I recommend you ask him to seek help. I definitely believe people can change but how much time of your life are you going to waste waiting on that change. Imagine the opportunities you have missed holding on to that abusive relationship. If you notice I didn't spend a lot of time trying to convince you to stay around. I said ask him to seek help. Better yet, I want you to seek help so you can leave. No woman deserves to be treated like a slave or a punching bag. I don't even want to try to convince you to stay in an abusive relationship, so you talk to a counselor or relative, even seek help from your local police department. Do whatever it takes for you to get yourself out of that relationship.

Let's not forget that **all abuse doesn't have to be physical.** In fact majority of abuse starts off mental. Your man keeping you inside the house never taking you anywhere, that's mental abuse. Does your man always go out with his boys and leave you home with the kids, and every time you think about going out he gives you some excuse on why you shouldn't. Now when your girls want you to go out for some reason you just don't like to go out anymore. That's because your man has mentally abused you to the point where you think that it's not good for you to go out. The excuses will keep coming. They were shooting at that club, nothing but kids there, or the famous, it was so horrible tonight. He's trying to convince you that he didn't have fun and if you would've gone out, you would've been wasting your time. Let's be for real; he met you at the club. That's just a small example of mental abuse. Have you ever tried on an outfit that he used to like you in when he first met you, now it just doesn't look right? This mental abuse tactic is to lower your self-esteem. This way you won't have the confidence to ever leave him for someone else.

Ladies I recommend that you go out. Sometimes it's good to go out and hear a compliment from another person especially when your own man doesn't compliment you enough. Go out and let someone remind you of how beautiful you are. This is exactly why it's important to have your own life when you're in a relationship. Don't ever base your whole world around your man. It's okay to want to please your man but never spoil him too much. Trust me, he will take advantage and that's where the abuse can begin.

So have your own money, car, house

if you not married, friends and hobbies, it will be more beneficial for you than you know it. Doing this it will keep balance in your relationship and your man will definitely respect you more. Women make the mistake of letting a man know that he has her heart completely. Unless you are sure he is the one you plan to spend the rest of your life with and he's already proven to you that he is loyal and is just as much in love with you as you are with him; keep him guessing.

When a man knows he has your heart, he's more confident that you're not going anywhere. Therefore, he'll do several things to reassure what he knows. He may come in the house anytime he wants, demanding you to do things he knows you don't like. Like in the beginning you tell him; "I hate to be kissed on my ears". When you guys are making love where's the first place he kisses you? You guessed it, your ears! See he wants to feel special. He wants to know when it comes to him you have no morals or rules and when he sees that, he knows he got you. When a man know he's got you, that's when all the abuse and his **true self** start to show up in the relationship.

In this chapter you learned to leave immediately when your man starts to get abusive, mentally, or physically. Never base your whole world around your man. Never go against your values. You ever heard the saying if you stand for nothing you'll fall for anything?" That is so true, especially when it comes to relationship.

REMEMBER:

No woman deserves to be abused. It does not come with the territory of being in love. Be complete within yourself so if you ever run across an abusive man you can leave with no problem.

CHAPTER

4

HOW DO I

LEAVE HIM

WHEN I FEEL

I CAN'T LIVE

WITHOUT HIM

In this chapter I want you to recognize that no matter how much you think you love him, no matter how much you think you need him; you CAN live without him!

Well ladies this is one of the hardest things to do. When you're in a relationship that you know is wrong but you stick around because you can't see life without him. First step to this problem is most definitely having a great relationship with GOD. In order to leave someone that you are in love with, you are going to need **GOD's divine power.** Trust me, I have experienced it myself. Ask yourself; why do you think you're in love with him? Are you sure it's really love or are you just comfortable? How many women are with a man who they know is cheating, or very abusive? Better yet, how many women are with men who they know are way beneath their level? Plenty of women are, and this is usually **because the woman is not whole.**

It's so important to be whole as a woman. I have said this numerous times in this book, because when you're whole, you make better decisions. You don't have to be as bound to a relationship because you have your own. Nowadays women need to be very careful what you allow your man to do. In the beginning of the relationship the traditional way is for the man to pay for everything. The reason for this is because he's suppose to convince you that he can support you, but I recommend women to split the bill if you go out to eat, or on any date. I know a lot women may disagree. Some may say; **"if he take me out he better pay for me, I want me a sugar daddy, he better be a baller."** Apparently, what women don't understand is that there's a whole lot that comes behind him paying for dinner or anything else that he pays for. With every dollar he spends on you he's gaining more control on what he's trying to do. Majority of men main objective as we all know is to **get laid, have sex, screw, beat it up and smash**. Whatever lingo you use it's all the same. That is the first step,

The second step is to make you his bitch, what you mean his bitch? Okay he want you to be that woman who does whatever he want when he ask, but doesn't interfere with his normal life. Once you accept that, that's when the games begin. Now you're in this relationship with this man who's not in a relationship with you. Oh, but wait we have a problem; **he told you he love you,** and we all know you are so in love with him too, right? Not only are you in love with him but he got you in a committed relationship that he is not even in. What I mean is; he does whatever he wants to but doesn't allow you to do anything, and you listen; why? Because you're in love with him and you can't see your life without him.

WRONG! This is where you end it.

First thing you do is **stop answering his every call.** It's okay to make him think you busy sometimes even if the only thing you're doing is **watching your toenails dry.** As long as he's wondering why you're not answering his call you're in control.

Next step is for you to **keep yourself occupied** don't sit around the house depressed and bored, letting your heart and mind drive you crazy. **Do something different;** let's think about how much time and dedication you gave him. Now this is all your time and this is where a lot of women make their mistake. Instead of keeping yourself occupied **you sit at home and eat, or watch soap operas, reality shows, Oprah, or anything that will keep you in the house with no positive energy around you**. I say get up go to the gym, meet new people, go see family, anything to get you out of the house and around people.

Set a goal and not only set your goal, visualize your goal, **write it down** on a piece of paper, but you still not **done, speak it into existence.**

SAY THIS (and believe it)

- **I WILL GET OVER THIS MAN**

- **I WILL ACCOMPLISH ALL MY GOALS**

- **I WILL MEET NEW PEOPLE**

- **I WILL KEEP MYSELF OCCUPIED**

- **I WILL GO TO THE GYM**

- *AND MOST IMPORTANTLY**

- **I WILL GET A CLOSER RELATIONSHIP WITH GOD**

You do these things and all of a sudden you will realize, it's been a month and you haven't called or seen this man that you're "so called" in love with. I know it's easier said than done but this is all a process. I never said it will be easy. The hardest time is when **it's time to go to bed, WOOH!** Trust me I know. Like I said, I've been there. We already know that you need to have a great relationship with GOD.

God is first, but it's also okay **to have that friend on call** that is always there and really understands you and your whole situation. Now this friend can be your mom, dad, a relative, or maybe an ex-boyfriend who knows you and your circumstance quite well. It's imperative that your friend be strong, firm and real. You don't want or need a" **YES MAN,"** you know, someone who says yes to everything. They say what they know you want to hear. You want someone who's going to **tell you the real even if it hurts your feelings.** You need to be criticized on how you handle certain situations. That is extremely important.

Criticism is very much needed in all aspects of life because none of us are perfect in anything we do. I know this book needs a lot of criticism, but the content of this book justifies any mistakes I have made writing this book.

My point is, don't think you're the perfect woman and this won't happen to you. We all make mistakes especially when we're in love. When you're in love it's like you're living life with a blindfold, **you don't even recognize some of the things you do.** It's been months and he's still on my mind. **Well it is a process,** but instead of focusing on all the pain and negativity you feel; focus on the progress you've made. You use to starve yourself. Now you're eating three times a day. You never use to get any sleep. Now you're sleeping like a baby. **Do you see the progress?**

See a lot of people are more blessed then they think they are but they are so focused on the negative they don't even realize how good they got it. You got to be humble and more appreciative. You ever met someone who always complains about everything, but you look at them like, "man **your life is perfect."**

For example: A man gets into a car accident and completely totals his brand new car but no one was injured at all from the accident. The guy who totaled his car is highly upset. I mean steam is coming out of his ears. He gets out of the car ready to fight. Walks to the other vehicle and begins to yell scream and curses at the other driver. Saying things like; **"What the hell is wrong with you?** Did you see me turning? You blind asshole! I just bought this car, you son of a bitch! You better have full coverage insurance." Meanwhile the other driver gets out and says; "thank you Jesus my car is totaled and so is yours but I can run and jump. I don't have any injuries at all," and gives the angry man a hug. The angry man pushes the other driver and calls him crazy. In all reality the angry man is the one who's' crazy. Anytime you can walk away from an accident with no injuries, you're blessed. Your car can be replaced but your life can't. This is exactly what I mean when I say people focus on the negative instead of the positive. So instead of thinking about how bad things are, **focus on the positive.** This analogy is to show you the progress that you made and how to pay more attention to the positive and not the negative.

I always say find a positive out of every situation if it doesn't kill you. The reason you went through that is so you can **develop a certain type of strength in order to fulfill God's plan for your life.** A lot people say everything happens for a reason. I can agree with that but what people seem to forget is the decisions that we make determines what happens next. If you chose to stay in an abusive relationship with a man who is treating you so bad because you feel you just can't live without. **Don't think it's in God's plan for this man to destroy you.** We all have a free will and with every decision we make there's a path that follows it.

Okay let me get back to how to leave this man that you think you can't live without. I felt like I was preaching to you and lord knows I got a ways to go before I can be a preacher (but who knows). Let's say months have passed and still no contact has been made to this man. I guarantee he will be trying to contact you, because now **he's very confuse about how you're able to live without him.**

One thing I can assure you is this; if you know you can't live without him **then he definitely knows that you can't live**

without him. So for him to see something different in you as far as how you treat him will definitely open his eyes. **He will start doing things you never thought he would do.** Like I said earlier in the book a man doesn't want you to know how much he really cares about you. Once he sees you're really fed up and you really trying to let go, that's when his real feelings will come out and **he'll try to be the perfect man for you.** Hopefully you kill two birds with one stone; not only do you make him change and he begins to show you how he really feel, but also, you'll get over him and now **you're strong enough to live without him.**

REMEMBER

You want someone who's going to tell you the real even if it hurts your feelings. You need to be criticized on how you handle certain situations.

HE LOVES ME NOT

C
H
A
P
T
E
R

5

HOW DO I

MAKE

MY MAN

LOVE ME

In this chapter I want you to recognize that "one night stands" are a big, huge, gigantic mistake, especially if you want any kind of respectful future with this man. And the way to make him love you is to; MAKE HIM WAIT!

HE LOVES ME

Well we getting close to the end, but in this chapter I will basically review all the things we learned. I will also kind of put things in order for you on how to make your man love you. Mind you, everything you read from this book is my opinion and the things that I have discussed with you are either from **my own experiences or from people I have helped.** Note that I am a man with integrity, and I live for my respect so if I put any information in this book I believe in it and I will do my best to back up anything you learn from my book.

Let's speak on another major mistake women make with men. This is probably the most affective issue that will not allow any respect or balance in your relationship and that is **ONE NIGHT STANDS.** Never sleep with a man when you first meet him under **ANY** circumstances. I don't care if you think its love at first sight. I don't care if he's a preacher, or a famous celebrity. Once you sleep with a man the first time you meet him or just have a one night **stand he will never respect you.**

Yes! A man will say anything to get you home and he will be the **perfect man.** He's just doing all these things to get in your panties on the first night. By doing this he is immediately **putting you in a category**. Either you're wife material or you're just going to be one of his hoes. You will never be his lady or someone who he will treat with respect. **You will just be his bitch.** As soon as he sleeps with you he will automatically think you do this all the time. He will think this even if this is your first time having a one night stand or if he is someone that you've always liked.

The longer you wait to be intimate with a man the more respect he will have for you. This is where his trust begins. If you make a man wait 6 months before you ever have sex with him, he will respect you and trust you, he will give you freedom and love you the way you want to be love. Particularly, the longer you make him wait **the better he will be.** If you make a man wait over a year it's a good chance he will propose to you. The reason is because every man wants to feel special. He wants to know that everything you do is because he's special to you.

You heard the saying "lady in the streets but a freak in the sheets." That's so true; majority of every man wants that from his woman, but he wants to make sure that you're only a freak for him and not just any and every man. **Remember, he wants to feel special.** Now if you sleep with him on the first night you automatically disqualify yourself from being his girl, wife or anything that has respect associated with it (if he does respect you after a one night stand, this is not a man that you want to be with anyway. If he wants to be with you or feels he loves you after a one night stand, what makes you think he won't go and fall in love with another woman after a one night stand).

Men believe women who sleep with them on the first night have no morals or respect. Those women are the one's guys introduce to their boy who just got out a prison from doing a bid. His boy gets out and says: "I need a slut for the night, it's been 5years." Well, "one night stand girl" you're the one he will be calling. Now, is this the category you want to be under? So trust me, **one night stands are the worst.**

See when you make a man wait, that makes him feel like **you're one in a million.**

Almost every man has had a one night stand but **how many men can say my girl made me wait** a whole year or even 6 months before we had sex. Do you know the power and respect in that? Just for making him wait that long he will have so much respect for you. **He will treat you like a queen and will try his hardest to keep you happy.**

Now don't get me wrong by doing this you let him know you will never cheat on him so sometimes he begins to search for his side chicks. He got his wife you the good woman who made him wait a year, now he got to place his side chicks in order. So I recommend that you let him know that at any given moment **he can lose you!**

Now, it's up to you to keep the spice in the relationship. Make sure you cook him a good meal every day. Give him massages and it is also great when you automatically know where he's hurting. Another thing is to remember to be you alter ego keep your sex life exciting. Don't be afraid to give him oral sex and make sexy sounds while you're doing it. Men love that sound. Sometimes the sound women make can be more intense than the actual feeling itself. **TRUST ME, THIS IS VERY IMPORTANT! I know it's a little raw** but I want you to keep your relationship and your man at home and away from the one night stand women who wants to sink their claws into him.

Keep your figure together and sometimes even watch adult films to learn new tricks for your man, he will love that. Make sure you clean up good not only the house but yourself. **Have nice smelling fragrances all over your body** so that anywhere he smells that fragrance he will think of you. Keep your vagina fresh at all times. When you guys go out, keep your fashion up to date. Pay attention to the styles that are in at the time. Look at what Be'yonce or the Kardashian's and plenty other famous celebrities are wearing. All these things will keep your man happy and so much in love with you. You do this and he has no reason to ever cheat on you because what you are doing is becoming his everything all in one.

So many men keep a variety of women because they all have different qualities that he enjoys, but if you can do all these by yourself I can assure you that he will put a ring on your finger. He will be singing **"Ain't No Woman Like The One I Got,"** and if he's singing this song then you have nothing to worry about.

REMEMBER

Men believe women who sleep with them on the first night have no morals or respect.

AND THESE ARE THE TEN WAYS TO MAKE YOUR MAN LOVE YOU

- **SET YOUR DEMANDS EARLY**

- **BE WHOLE AS A WOMAN, HAVING YOUR OWN LIFE AND FRIENDS**

- **HAVE A CHECKLIST AND A PREFERENCE FOR WHAT YOU WANT IN YOUR MAN**

- **NEVER SLEEP WITH A MAN YOU REALLY LIKE WITHOUT BECOMING HIS WOMAN FIRST**

- **NEVER LET A MAN CALL YOU A BITCH YOU MUST DEMAND YOUR RESPECT**

- **PAY ATTENTION TO THE TEST THAT HE PUT YOU THROUGH, AND ACE THEM WITH FLYING COLORS**

- **NEVER LET A MAN ABUSE YOU PHYSICALLY OR MENTALLY**

- **NO! AND I MEAN NO! ONE NIGHT STANDS**

- **CHEAT ON YOUR MAN WITH YOUR MAN**

- **MOST IMPORTANTLY HAVE A GREAT RELATIONSHIP WITH GOD.**

LADIES; THIS IS YOUR BIBLE, YOUR WEAPON AGAINST, HEARTACHE, HEARTBREAK, AND DEFINITELY ABUSE. CARRY IT AT ALL TIMES, EITHER IN YOUR HEART OR IN YOUR PURSE. IT IS TRUTH AND IT WILL:

MAKE YOU FREE!

C
H
A
P
T
E
R

6

MY

APOLOGY

TO

GOD

This is the last chapter to my book and it's very important to me. This is about me and the mistakes I made trying to figure out this thing called life.

Confessions of A Cheater

Today I am a 30 year old man with 4 kids by 4 different women. I have a 12 year old daughter who I am extremely proud of, a 10 year old son who is the most protective person I know, a 7 year old who I'm still trying to figure out what he wants to be who is currently living with me, and a 2month old who just got over RSV.

I thank God that he is over that because now his personality is starting to come out. I don't consider any of my kids a mistake because I am a firm believer of God and know that he's the reason certain things happen the way they do. I go by the saying **when life gives you lemons make lemonade** and that's what I've been doing all my life.

See a lot of people know me by what they hear and what they see. If you ask ten people in my city to describe me (Vincent), you'd probably hear something like this. He is a good dresser, takes care of his kids, very respectful, a gamer, loves to gamble, not violent but he has gun permit, he go to community college and has a nice truck.

Okay those are the good things then the bad things; he's a player, been with a lot of women, always late, always gambling on poker or anything, puts money before anything, sometimes he's too nice, let people take advantage of his kindness, and some other things that we might not need to put in this book. **But, no one really knows how truly I love God** (maybe a selective few).

I grew up in church. I can honestly say that my dad was in my life and I have to thank him for introducing me to God at an early age. I use to hate going to church. I mean who doesn't when you're a kid. Church didn't start getting interesting to me until I was about 10 to 13 years of age.

My mom really wasn't a church going woman she was a gambler and I mean gambler. But I can't only blame her because her mom was a gambler. Deloris Faye Williams, God rest her soul, my granny. We use to play card games for a quarter when I was 8 years old. So gambling has been in me from the womb. 3247 Kimball Toledo Ohio, that's my granny house. That's where you learned everything. My granny had 18 children, 11 boys and 7 girls so you can imagine how crowded her house was. I mean it was so packed we didn't even have a house key.

Out of the 18 kids my granny had, the majority were hustlers and gang members. **Later on a selective few turned their life over to God**, but they were mostly in the streets. So that's my mom's side of the family.

My dad's side is the complete opposite. 80% of my dad's side is Christians, and I mean faithfully. Not just on Sundays, I'm talking about Monday prayer meeting, Tuesday Deacon studies, Wednesday Bible study, Friday youth choir, Saturday mass choir, Sunday devotion Sunday afternoon regular service then second service. Later on that night was a concert. You get my drift, from one side of my family I learned about God and from the other side I learned about the streets. **What it created within me was a very respectful and intelligent monster,** and I wouldn't change it because it made me who I am.

I love my church family even though we lost touch: Reverend Williams, Reverend Stillman, Deacon Stegall and Mrs Stegall Mrs Campbell, Patti, Deloris, Sandy, Joy, Suge. Then my crew Donnel John and Shon, Vale, Pat, Veda, Drea, Qual, and the twins but how can I forget Alisha. I kind of have to thank her for being at our church because she was the reason I was going. She was tall, light skinned, bow legged, long hair and just beautiful to me. And **she's what kept me going to church until I started to understand what the preacher was saying.** Once that happened I found my own reason to go to church.

Our church was called Christian Love Missionary Baptist Church and I loved my church family. I don't know what happen but somehow we all split up. That's when I decided to spend time with the other side of my family. The things I learned were very interesting. I learned how to become a hustler, a player, and to have a good sense of fashion. I learned how to camouflage with the streets.

No matter what I did, God never left my heart. You know how many times there have been fights with my family and I didn't do anything? People always thought I was scared but what they didn't know was, what God put in my heart as a youth is something that no one can ever change. I was never scared because there were times I could have helped stomp people to the ground without any harm coming my way. I chose not to because I always said **"what goes around comes right back around."** Even though they don't know who is stomping them, God knows.

Everyone has a path and freewill and our path changes every day with the decision we make. I always wonder what I would be doing right now if my church would've never broken up. I figure this path I walk everyday now was something I needed to do in order to be able to communicate with a certain group of people and get through to them.

I believe my life is a testimony and I remember saying when I was 14 I will become a preacher one day. Who knows when, but one day? People wonder how I do things and never get into trouble or how I don't have any felonies or why I never had a broken bone or a stitch. I say God loves me and I know he has favor over me. Sometime it's scary to think that I'm taking advantage of God's love because of some of the choices I make, but this life we live gets so hard at times.

Every day of my life I say this prayer to God; **Lord thank you for waking me up this morning. Please forgive all my sins. Lord please let it be continuous of me saying thank you all day because I can't thank you enough. Lord bless my mom, dad, kids, family, friends and the things I don't say in this prayer that I didn't know to say or should have said please add to my prayer in Jesus name I pray Amen.** Now I don't know if that prayer has protected me for all these years or not. But I never try to forget to say it.

My apology to God is because I have made plenty mistakes as we all have. But I feel guilty because I know better. I knew to do right at a young age. I grew up and tried to put God aside and make my own choices. Those choices got me 4 kids with 4 different women a one bedroom apartment a lot of clothes a truck and a Owens Community College education. Not to put a knock on Owens but I 'm not even done with that yet.

I have hurt lots of women in my life and I blame it on me being selfish and not listening to the God that's in my heart. One thing I can say is I was never a thief and I always try to be honest even when I lie (if that makes any sense at all). A lot people wonder why I am so giving. People think it's because I have it to give. **NO! I don't!** How can I give anything when I got four mouths to feed? I give because I feel that's what God wants me to do. This life I live I feel if I don't help others, God will punish me. So I continue to let people take advantage even when I can see it plain as day.

God I want to apologize for all the decisions that I made. I know it isn't over **but Lord please help me guide my steps in a better direction** In Jesus Name Amen.

Sometimes I wonder if it's okay to speak about God so much when I know I'm not living the way I'm supposed to. Then I remember God saying come as you are. A lot people feel he's saying you can wear whatever you want to church. But I believe he's saying come to me as you are despite having 4 kids and no wife. Despite being in the streets and despite the sins you've committed. See, we as a people feel we will make that change one day. You know; as soon as we get **everything** in order. Trust me when I tell you that will never happen. That's just the devil deceiving you.

You have to come to God with all your sins and all your problems because he is the only one that can pull you out of them. Doesn't it seem like every time you're ready to spend more time with God something comes up that you know is wrong but you love to do it. The devil is a lie, he will put thoughts in your head and plant a seed in you and watch it grow until he destroys you. That's why it's so important to have a great relationship with God so you can recognize Lucifer's evil games. I'm not sitting here telling you guys I am a saint, not at all. Hell, I haven't even read the whole Bible yet. What I am telling you is that if you ever see me and you ever wonder why I am the way that I am, now you know. **I'm in a war for my life**. Hopefully this book will send me better guidance and more understanding on how to defeat the things that have trapped me for so many years.

I thank you God for protecting me and ask you to don't give up on me yet. This Book is my apology to **YOU LORD**, for all the women I hurt and the terrible judgments

I made. **I pray this book helps every woman and man.** I also hope that it leads more people to God and know this; **"it's NOT over until it's over."**

My Prayer

Lord thank you for waking up whoever is reading this book this morning. I ask you to please forgive all of their sins. Please bless their parents, family and friends. Please allow them to continue to praise and thank you all day. Assure them that they can't thank you enough and that the things that are not added in this prayer that should have been said you have already added them. In Jesus name we pray; Amen.

HE LOVES ME NOT

I LOVE MYSELF

COMING SOON!!!!!!!!!!!

Confessions of A Cheater 2 (The True Story)

&

Undercover Mafia

By yours truly….. Mr. V. Williams